Hamlyn
low-fat
Cooking

Contents

NOTES

- All the recipes in this book have been analysed by a professional nutritionist, so that you can see their nutritional content at a glance. The abbreviations are as follows:
  Kcal = calories
  KJ = kilojoules
  CHO = carbohydrate.
  The analysis refers to each portion.

- Both metric and imperial measurements have been given in all recipes. Use one set of measurements only and not a mixture of both.

- Standard level spoon measurements are used in all recipes.
  1 tablespoon = one 15 ml spoon
  1 teaspoon = one 5 ml spoon

- Eggs should be medium to large unless otherwise stated.

- Milk should be skimmed unless otherwise stated.

- Meat and poultry should be cooked thoroughly. To test if poultry is cooked, pierce the flesh through the thickest part with a skewer or fork – the juices should run clear, never pink or red. Do not re-freeze poultry that has been frozen previously and thawed.

- Do not re-freeze a dish that has been frozen previously.

- Pepper should be freshly ground black pepper unless otherwise stated.

- Fresh herbs should be used, unless otherwise stated. If unavailable, use dried herbs as an alternative but halve the quantities stated.

- Measurements for canned food have been given as a standard metric equivalent.

- Ovens should be preheated to the specified temperature – if using a fan-assisted oven, follow the manufacturer's instructions for adjusting the time and the temperature.

Introduction

On a daily basis it is wise to keep clear of highly fatty foods and increase your intake of foods high in protein and carbohydrates. Fats are high in calories and can contribute to some extent to weight problems. The incidence of coronary heart disease has increased dramatically in the past 50 years or so, and medical research has identified several major causes. One of these is too high a consumption of saturated fats which may cause raised blood cholesterol; meat and dairy products are the worst offenders, but the consumption of these can be reduced and there are many other delicious foods that can be eaten in their place. We aim to show you here that this doesn't necessarily mean missing out on flavour or compromising on nutrition, it just means adopting a slightly different approach to choosing and using foods – selecting healthy ingredients, using herbs, spices and flavourings to add flavour and not fat, and marinating food before cooking in wine, herbs, spices and garlic.

Fat

Fat adds moisture to food so it is essential that when cooking without it, the food doesn't dry out. This can be done by covering with foil, or basting with stock or water so that the food almost steams and the natural flavours come through. Herbs and spices can also be used to add flavour without adding fat.

Oils – olive oil and rapeseed oil are high in monounsaturated fats, which may help to protect against heart disease. In addition, rapeseed oil is high in vitamin E.

Spray oils – these are excellent when frying as it is easier to use less oil than from a bottle. Look for extra virgin olive oil spray.

Low-fat spreads – these contain a high proportion of water and are not suitable for cooking but they are an excellent substitute to margarine and butter for reducing calories and total fat intake. Do check the fat content on the packaging.

Dairy Produce

Dairy products such as milk, butter, cream, cheese and ice cream are one of the main sources of saturated fats. Sometimes all that is needed is to replace the usual products that you buy with low-fat alternatives.

Skimmed milk – this is fresh cows' milk with a fat content of no more than 0.3% (often 0.1%). This milk is therefore ideal for anyone wishing to cut down on their fat intake. It is not suitable for babies and children as the fat soluble vitamins A and D are removed with the fat, although other nutrient levels remain the same. The milk looks thin and can be used in tea and coffee as well as in soups, sauces and cakes.

Semi-skimmed milk – this has a fat content of 1.5–1.8% and tastes less rich than full-cream milk.

Smatana – this is a soured cream made from skimmed milk, single cream and a souring culture, making it a good low-fat substitute for cream. It

should be added towards the end of the cooking time and not allowed to boil as it will curdle.

Crème fraîche – this is a cream that has been treated with a culture that gives it a light acidity without sourness. It is an important ingredient in French cooking. Use low-fat crème fraîche wherever possible.

Low-fat yogurt – made from concentrated skimmed milk, this has between 0.5 and 2% fat. If possible use very low fat yogurt which contains less than 0.5% fat.

Quark – a fresh curd cheese made throughout Germany from cows' milk. The variety made with skimmed milk contains the least fat. Quark is white, with a spoonable texture and delicate sour taste.

Edam – this is a semi-hard cheese from Holland which is well known for its red wax coat and ball shape. It is made from pasteurized skimmed cows' milk and is low in calories. Edam is golden yellow with a supple texture, a sparse scattering of holes and a nutty taste.

Full-fat soft cheese – this is lower in fat than cream cheese, both are unripened cows' milk cheese made from cream. It is soft and white with a smooth texture. It is often used to make cheesecakes.

Cottage cheese – this is a white, granular cheese with a clean, mild taste. It is available plain or flavoured with herbs, fruit or vegetables. It is also available in low-fat varieties. Cottage cheese is a type of curd cheese made from skimmed cows' milk.

Virtually fat-free fromage frais – this is fresh curd cheese made from pasteurized skimmed cows' milk. Its consistency varies from soft, light and pourable to relatively thick and firm. The flavour is mildly acidic and the fat content is almost nil.

Cream substitutes – there are a number of cream substitutes on the market made from vegetable fats and water. These are lower in fat than real cream but have an inferior taste.

Light mozzarella – mozzarella is an unripened cheese from Italy which was originally made from buffaloes' milk. Nowadays cows' milk is more commonly used. Mozzarella is white and spongy with a mild, creamy-sour taste and is traditionally shaped into balls. The low-fat variety is often labelled 'light'.

Low-fat cheeses – some cheeses such as Cheddar and Cheshire can be bought labelled 'reduced fat'. These are made in a similar way to traditional hard cheeses but with about half the fat content; low-fat cheeses tend to have a milder flavour than full-fat cheeses.

Meat

Try to limit portions of red meat to 75 g/3 oz and choose the leanest cuts possible whenever you can. Remove all traces of visible fat before cooking the meat. If mince is required, it is better to buy very lean cuts of steak, such as sirloin, and mince it yourself or get your butcher to do this for you. If you buy prepacked mince it is difficult to tell how much fat there actually is. When roasting meat, always place a rack in the bottom of the roasting tin so that the meat does not actually sit in its own juices. Grilling and griddling are much healthier methods of cooking meat than frying as no extra fat is needed.

Poultry and game – such as rabbit, venison, pigeon, partridge and pheasant, are nearly always a lot lower in fat than red meat and contain more polyunsaturated fat and less saturated fat than other meats. Chicken and turkey are a lot leaner than goose and duck, though the fat is less saturated than in red meats. Most of the fat in poultry is found just beneath the skin, so it is advisable always to use lean parts of the bird, such as the breast, and to remove the skin and trim away any visible fat.

Fish and Shellfish

Fish is an excellent source of protein and very low in fat. White fish such as cod, coley, haddock, whiting and skate are low in fat. Fatty fish, such as mackerel, herring, sardines, tuna, salmon and trout are all excellent sources of polyunsaturated oils. If using canned fish, such as tuna, sardines and salmon, choose ones that have been preserved in brine or spring water rather than oil. Steaming, poaching and microwaving are all excellent methods of cooking fresh fish without the addition of fat. Steaming or baking fish in parcels of greaseproof paper or foil with herbs and flavourings is an ideal method of cooking as it seals in all the flavour. Many shellfish including prawns, lobster and crab are very low in fat although prawns actually contain a higher level of cholesterol, weight for weight, than meat and poultry.

Fruits, Vegetables and Grains

Fruit provides a ready source of energy because it is rich in natural sugar (fructose), and minerals and vitamins are present in most fruit. Fruit is also a good source of dietary fibre and low in calories. Choose from fruit is season such as apples, bananas, strawberries, raspberries, apricots, cherries, currants, grapes and kiwi fruit. Vegetables are very important to a balanced diet. They provide minerals, vitamins and fibre and some such as potatoes and parsnips provide carbohydrate. Some vegetables such as pulses provide protein, but most vegetables are low in protein and low in fat. Olives and avocados are the exception as they are both high in fat. There are an enormous variety of exotic vegetables and salads available and they can be prepared in innumerable ways. Pulses are rich in protein, carbohydrate and vitamins and minerals. They are also inexpensive and extremely versatile. Fresh pasta contains eggs which adds extra fat so for a low-fat diet use dried pasta which just contains durum wheat and water. Wholewheat pasta is healthier as it contains the whole wheat grain, which provides more protein and fibre. Rice supplies many important nutrients and minerals such as potassium and phosphorus.

Nuts and Seeds

These are high in fat and calories. They are cholesterol free and their fat is unsaturated.

Foods to avoid

Highly processed foods such as crisps and snacks, biscuits and cakes, tend to contain a lot of fat and so do processed meats, sausages and mayonnaise. As a rule fresh fruit and vegetables and freshly prepared foods are the best choice.

Low-fat Cooking Techniques

Poaching, steaming, baking in foil, stir-frying, microwaving, grilling, griddling and barbecuing are all excellent low-fat cooking methods, rather than deep- and shallow-frying and roasting. It is a good idea to use non-stick saucepans and woks so less fat is needed.

Homemade Stocks

Nothing beats the flavour of homemade stock if you have the time. Also by making your own, you can monitor your fat intake more accurately. The following are high flavour but low fat stocks:

Vegetable Stock

3 potatoes, chopped
1 onion, sliced
2 leeks, chopped
2 celery sticks, chopped
2 carrots, chopped
1 small fennel head,
    thinly sliced
few sprigs of thyme
few parsley stalks
2 bay leaves
salt and pepper

1 Put all the vegetables into a saucepan with the herbs and 1.5 litres/2 ½ pints water. Bring to the boil slowly, then skim.

2 Add salt and pepper to taste. Simmer, covered, for about 1 ½ hours. Skim the stock 3–4 times during cooking.

3 Strain the stock through clean muslin or a very fine sieve. Cool quickly and store in the refrigerator until required.

Makes about 1 litre/1¾ pints

Fish Stock

1 kg/2 lb fish trimmings
1 small onion, finely
    chopped
2 leeks, chopped
1 bay leaf
few parsley stalks
few sprigs of fennel
large piece of lemon rind
200 ml/7 fl oz dry white wine
salt and pepper

1 Place the fish trimmings in a large saucepan with the onion, leeks, bay leaf, parsley, fennel, lemon rind and 1.5 litres/2 ½ pints water. Slowly bring to the boil, then skim any surface scum.

2 Add the white wine, and salt and pepper to taste and simmer very gently for 30 minutes, skimming the stock once or twice during cooking.

3 Strain the stock through clean muslin or a very fine sieve. Cool quickly and store in the refrigerator until required.

Makes about 1 litre/1¾ pints

Chicken Stock

1 chicken carcass,
plus giblets
1 onion, chopped
2 large carrots, chopped
1 celery stick, chopped
1 bay leaf
few parsley stalks
1 thyme sprig
salt and pepper

1 Remove any skin or fat from the chicken carcass and chop into small pieces. Place in a large saucepan with the giblets, onions, carrots, celery, bay leaf, parsley stalks, thyme and 1.8 litres/3 pints of water.

2 Bring to the boil and skim, removing any scum or fat that remains on the surface. Lower the heat and simmer for 2–2 ½ hours, skimming the stock once or twice during cooking.

3 Strain the stock through clean muslin or a very fine sieve. Cool quickly and store in the refrigerator until required.

Makes about 1 litre/1¾ pints

These simple, eye-catching soups and starters include refreshing chilled soups. The chunkier soups could be served with bread to make a satisfying, healthy lunch.

soups and starters

yellow pepper
soup

Serves	**5**
Preparation time	**15–20** minutes
Cooking time	**50–55** minutes
Kcal	**100**
KJ	**425**
Protein	**2** g
Fat	**5** g
CHO	**11** g

**3 yellow peppers, cored
and deseeded**

**50 g/2 oz butter or
margarine**

1 small onion, chopped

**1.2 litres/2 pints Vegetable
Stock (see page 6)**

**1 teaspoon mild curry
powder**

¼ teaspoon turmeric

**1 tablespoon chopped
fresh coriander, or
1 teaspoon dried leaf
coriander**

**300 g/10 oz potatoes,
peeled and chopped**

salt

1 Chop one pepper finely and place it in a small saucepan, then chop the remaining peppers roughly.

2 Melt 25 g/1 oz of the butter or margarine in another saucepan and cook the onion and roughly chopped peppers for 5 minutes, stirring frequently. Stir in the stock, curry powder, turmeric and coriander, season with salt, then add the potatoes. Bring to the boil, then lower the heat and simmer, partially covered, for 40–45 minutes, or until the vegetables are very soft.

3 Melt the remaining butter with the finely chopped pepper in the small pan. Cook over a gentle heat until the pepper is very soft. Reserve for the garnish.

4 Purée the onion, pepper and potato mixture in batches in a blender or food processor until very smooth. Return to a clean saucepan and reheat gently, taste and adjust the seasoning if necessary. Serve in warmed soup plates or bowls, garnished with a little of the sautéed chopped yellow pepper.

Sweet yellow peppers are milder in
flavour than green ones. All peppers
are rich in vitamin C.

Choose broad beans with soft, tender pale green pods with a satiny 'bloom'. The beans inside should be small and not fully mature.

bean and
mushroom soup

6	Serves
15–20 minutes	Preparation time
about **30** minutes	Cooking time
227	Kcal
962	KJ
15 g	Protein
5 g	Fat
33 g	CHO

125 g/4 oz dried haricot
beans, soaked overnight
and drained

125 g/4 oz dried red kidney
beans, soaked overnight
and drained

2 tablespoons oil

1 onion, sliced

1 garlic clove, crushed

125 g/4 oz button
mushrooms, sliced

1.2 litres/2 pints Vegetable
Stock (see page 6)

175 g/6 oz broad beans,
shelled

50 g/2 oz dried pasta,
such as radiatori

salt and pepper

1 Place the haricot and red kidney beans in separate saucepans, cover with cold water and bring to the boil. Simmer the haricot beans for 1½ hours and the kidney beans for 1 hour or until tender, adding salt towards the end of cooking.

2 Heat the oil in a large saucepan, add the onion and cook for about 5 minutes until soft. Add the garlic, mushrooms, vegetable stock, broad beans and season to taste with salt and pepper and simmer for 10 minutes. Stir in the pasta and the drained haricot and kidney beans and simmer for a further 15 minutes or until the pasta is al dente.

spaghetti
with clam sauce

Serves	**4**
Preparation time	**15** minutes
Cooking time	about **30** minutes
Kcal	**370**
KJ	**1566**
Protein	**22** g
Fat	**2** g
CHO	**66** g

400 g/13 oz can tomatoes

4 tablespoons dry red or
white wine

2 tablespoons finely
chopped parsley

2 teaspoons finely
chopped basil

1 small onion, finely chopped

2 garlic cloves, crushed

250–300 g/8–10 oz
dried spaghetti

300 g/10 oz can baby clams,
well drained

salt and pepper

chopped parsley, to garnish

1 Place the canned tomatoes with their juice in a food processor or blender. Add the wine and herbs and work to a purée.

2 Heat a wok or heavy saucepan and dry fry the onion for 3–6 minutes, turning constantly. Add the garlic and puréed tomatoes. Season to taste. Cover and simmer gently for about 15 minutes, stirring occasionally.

3 Meanwhile, bring a large saucepan of salted water to the boil. Add the spaghetti, stir and cook for 10–12 minutes until al dente.

4 Stir the clams into the tomato sauce and heat them through. Adjust the seasoning if necessary. Drain the spaghetti well and turn it into a warmed serving bowl. Pour over the sauce and garnish with chopped parsley. Serve at once.

The Italian for this dish is *Spaghetti alle Vongole*. It is traditionally made with small fresh clams but using canned clams makes this a speedy dish.

chilled stuffed
artichokes

Serves	**4**
Preparation time	**20** minutes, plus cooling
Cooking time	about **35** minutes
Kcal	**133**
KJ	**558**
Protein	**9** g
Fat	**3** g
CHO	**17** g

**4 artichokes, stems
trimmed and top third of
leaves removed**
1 tablespoon lemon juice
**Steamed Vegetables with
Ginger (see right)**

sauce:
150 g/5 oz tofu, drained
**4 tablespoons tomato
purée**
**4 tablespoons horseradish
sauce**
2 teaspoons lemon juice
2 teaspoons white vinegar
½ teaspoon onion salt
½ teaspoon sugar
few drops Tabasco sauce
**½ teaspoon grated
lemon rind**
**freshly ground white
pepper, to taste**

1 Place the artichokes and lemon juice in a deep saucepan and add boiling water to cover. Cover and cook for 30 minutes, or until one of the artichoke leaves pulls off easily. Remove from the pan, turn upside down to drain, then refrigerate to cool.

2 Remove the central choke of each artichoke and fill with chilled Steamed Vegetables with Ginger (see right).

3 To make the sauce, place all the ingredients in a blender or food processor and purée. Pour some sauce over each artichoke to serve.

steamed vegetables with ginger:

Place 3 carrots, cut into rounds, 4 tablespoons tomato purée, 75 g/3 oz each cauliflower and broccoli florets, 2 small courgettes, cut into rounds, and 3.5 cm/1 ½ inch piece root ginger, peeled and cut into thin strips, in a medium saucepan and steam for 7 minutes until tender.

Lean cuts of meat and poultry can be simply grilled for quick, low-fat meals. What makes these dishes special is an imaginative use of herbs, spices and flavourings.

meat and chicken dishes

green chilli
chicken with spinach taglioni

Serves	**4**
Preparation time	**10** minutes
Cooking time	**20** minutes
Kcal	**355**
KJ	**1423**
Protein	**25** g
Fat	**5** g
CHO	**50** g

**4 boneless, skinless
chicken breasts,
each about 75 g/3 oz**
1 teaspoon olive oil
**2 green chillies,
deseeded and sliced**
**1 green pepper, cored,
deseeded and sliced**
1 teaspoon lime juice
**400 g/13 oz can
chopped tomatoes**
**15 g/½ oz pitted
black olives**
**15 g/½ oz pitted
green olives**
**250 g/8 oz dried spinach
taglioni**
salt and pepper
**flat leaf parsley sprigs,
to garnish**

1 Cut each chicken breast into 4 pieces. Heat a wok or large frying pan and add the oil; when it is hot, add the chicken pieces, chillies and green pepper. Stir-fry for about 5 minutes or until the chicken has browned.

2 Stir in the lime juice, tomatoes and olives, with salt and pepper to taste. Reduce the heat and simmer the sauce for 15 minutes.

3 Meanwhile, bring a large saucepan of salted water to the boil. Add the pasta, stir and cook for about 10–12 minutes, until al dente.

4 Drain the pasta. Pile it on to a large warmed platter and spoon over the chicken mixture. Garnish with flat leaf parsley sprigs and serve at once.

To remove the seeds from the chillies; cut the chilli in half lengthways with a small, sharp knife and scrape out the seeds. For a hotter dish, leave the seeds in place.

Sugar snap peas can be used instead of
the mangetout; they have a more rounded
pod and sweeter flavour.

beef
and mangetout stir-fry

4	Serves
10 minutes, plus marinating	Preparation time
8 minutes	Cooking time
348	Kcal
1475	KJ
27 g	Protein
5 g	Fat
50 g	CHO

25 g/1 oz fresh root ginger,
 peeled and shredded
1 garlic clove, crushed
4 tablespoons light soy
 sauce
2 tablespoons dry sherry
1 teaspoon chilli sauce
1 teaspoon clear honey
½ teaspoon Chinese
 five-spice powder
375 g/12 oz fillet steak,
 finely sliced
250 g/8 oz dried low-fat
 egg noodles
250 g/8 oz mangetout,
 trimmed
salt and pepper
shredded spring onions,
 to garnish

1 Combine the ginger, garlic, soy sauce, sherry, chilli sauce, honey and five-spice powder in a non-metallic bowl. Stir well. Add the steak, stir to coat thoroughly, then cover and marinate for at least 30 minutes.

2 Bring a large saucepan of lightly salted water to the boil. Add the noodles, remove the pan from the heat, cover and leave to stand for 5 minutes.

3 Meanwhile, heat a wok or frying pan. Add 2 tablespoons of the marinade and the beef and stir-fry for about 3–6 minutes.

4 Add the mangetout and the remaining marinade to the wok, with salt and pepper if required. Stir-fry for a further 2 minutes.

5 Drain the noodles and arrange them in warmed serving bowls. Spoon the stir-fry over the top, garnish with shredded spring onions and serve.

chinese pork
with bamboo shoots

Serves	**4**
Preparation time	**15** minutes
Cooking time	**20** minutes
Kcal	**219**
KJ	**913**
Protein	**19** g
Fat	**14** g
CHO	**6** g

2 tablespoons groundnut oil

300 g/10 oz lean pork, shredded

1 small Chinese cabbage, shredded

1 tablespoon coarsely chopped hazelnuts

250 g/8 oz bamboo shoots, drained and sliced, with juices reserved

2 tablespoons soy sauce

1 teaspoon curry powder

pinch of chilli powder

small pinch of sugar

salt and pepper

1 Heat the oil in a non-stick frying pan or wok, add the pork and stir-fry quickly until lightly browned. Season with salt and pepper to taste.

2 Add the cabbage, nuts and a few tablespoons of liquid from the can of bamboo shoots. Cook, stirring, for about 5 minutes.

3 Add the bamboo shoots, soy sauce, curry powder, chilli powder and sugar and mix well. Cook gently for a further 10 minutes. Serve immediately.

Bamboo shoots are a popular ingredient in Chinese dishes. In China, raw shoots are used, but the canned variety are a good substitute.

Fish needs only simple preparation and a few extra ingredients to make a really exciting meal. It cooks quickly and is naturally low in fat and high in flavour.

fish
dishes

Serve this delicious dish with steamed new potatoes and mangetout or sugar snap peas.

poached salmon
with hot basil sauce

4	Serves
20 minutes	Preparation tim
13 minutes	Cooking time
185	Kcal
784	KJ
23 g	Protein
3 g	Fat
11 g	CHO

1 large bunch of fresh basil

2 celery sticks, chopped

1 carrot, chopped

1 small courgette, chopped

1 small onion, chopped

4 salmon steaks, about
**   50 g/2 oz each**

75 ml/3 fl oz white wine

125 ml/4 fl oz water

1 teaspoon lemon juice

15 g/½ oz unsalted butter

salt and pepper

basil sprigs, to garnish

1 Strip the leaves off half the basil and set aside.

2 Spread the chopped celery, carrot, courgette and onion evenly over the bottom of a large flameproof dish or pan with a lid, place the salmon steaks on top and cover them with the remaining basil.

3 Pour over the wine and water and add salt and pepper to taste. Bring to the boil, cover and simmer for about 10 minutes. Transfer the salmon to a warmed serving dish.

4 Bring the poaching liquid and vegetables back to the boil and simmer for 5 minutes. Strain into a blender or food processor and add the cooked and uncooked basil. Blend to a purée and transfer to a saucepan.

5 Bring the purée to the boil and reduce by half to thicken.

6 Remove the pan from the heat, add the lemon juice and stir in the butter. Pour the sauce over the salmon steaks and serve, garnished with basil sprigs.

trout in a paper bag

Serves	**4**
Preparation time	**30** minutes
Cooking time	**20** minutes
Kcal	**160**
KJ	**680**
Protein	**23** g
Fat	**5** g
CHO	**1** g

4 trout, about 125 g/4 oz each

2 garlic cloves,
finely chopped

1 tablespoon chopped thyme

1 tablespoon chopped
rosemary

150 ml/¼ pint rosé wine

salt and pepper

1 Cut 8 rectangles of greaseproof paper or kitchen foil, double the width of each trout, and half as long again as the fish.

2 Place 4 of the rectangles on a baking sheet. Lay a trout along the centre of each one, pull up the edges of the paper or foil and fold at each corner so that the paper forms a container for each fish.

3 Sprinkle a little salt and pepper, garlic and herbs over each trout, then spoon 2 tablespoons of the rosé wine over each one. Cover loosely with the remaining paper or foil and fold at the corners as before to form a lid over each fish. Fold the top and bottom layers of paper or foil together in several places. Bake the trout in a preheated oven, 190°C (375°F), Gas Mark 5, for 20 minutes, until the fish is cooked.

4 Take the fish to the table in the parcels to serve.

Thinly sliced courgettes, flavoured with crushed garlic and chopped fennel, can be wrapped in individual foil parcels and cooked with the fish. They make a delicious accompaniment.

fillets of sole
with melon and mint sauce

Serves	**4**
Preparation time	**20** minutes
Cooking time	**10–15** minutes
Kcal	**230**
KJ	**985**
Protein	**29** g
Fat	**3** g
CHO	**12** g

4 sole fillets, halved

2 tablespoons chopped mint

300 ml/½ pint dry
white wine

1 Charentais melon,
halved and seeded

150 ml/¼ pint natural
yogurt

salt and pepper

mint sprigs, to garnish

1 Season the sole fillets with salt and pepper and sprinkle with half of the mint. Roll up each fish fillet and secure with wooden cocktail sticks. Place the fish rolls in a deep frying pan and sprinkle over the remaining mint. Add the white wine. Cover the pan and poach gently for about 8 minutes, until the fish is tender.

2 Meanwhile, using a Parisian cutter or melon ball cutter, scoop the melon flesh into small balls. Cut out any remaining melon flesh attached to the skin.

3 Carefully drain the rolled fillets, place on a warm serving dish and keep warm. Remove the cocktail sticks.

4 Boil the poaching liquid with the remnants of melon flesh until well reduced and whisk until smooth. If necessary, purée in a food processor or blender.

5 Stir in the yogurt and heat the sauce through gently. Season with salt and pepper and spoon over the cooked fish. Garnish with the melon balls and sprigs of mint.

Charentais melon is a type of cantaloupe with a roughish, pale green skin. It has a fragrant orange flesh when ripe. Mint complements melon very well.

The huge variety of fresh vegetables available nowadays provides an opportunity for delicious and unusual recipes. Many of the recipes here are suitable for vegetarians.

vegetable dishes

chinese-style
vermicelli

Serves	**4**
Preparation time	**15** minutes
Cooking time	**20** minutes
Kcal	**320**
KJ	**1336**
Protein	**9** g
Fat	**5** g
CHO	**61** g

250 g/8 oz dried vermicelli

4 carrots, cut into fine matchsticks

4 courgettes, cut into fine matchsticks

125 g/4 oz small mangetout

5 teaspoons oil

4 spring onions, sliced diagonally

2.5 cm/1 inch piece of fresh root ginger, peeled and sliced into matchsticks

1–2 garlic cloves, crushed

4 tablespoons light soy sauce

1 tablespoon clear honey

1 tablespoon white wine vinegar

1 teaspoon coriander seeds, crushed

salt and pepper

parsley leaves, to garnish

1 Bring a large saucepan of salted water to the boil. Add the vermicelli, stir and bring back to the boil. Reduce the heat slightly and boil, uncovered, for 8–10 minutes, or until al dente, stirring occasionally.

2 Meanwhile, put the carrots, courgettes and mangetout into a colander or sieve and place over the pan of boiling vermicelli. Cover the colander and steam the vegetables for about 5 minutes until they are tender but still crunchy. Remove the colander and set it aside. Drain the vermicelli when it is still al dente.

3 Heat the oil in a wok or deep frying pan. Add the spring onions and ginger and cook gently, stirring, until the ingredients give off a spicy aroma. Add the garlic, soy sauce, honey, wine vinegar and coriander seeds, stirring well. Add the vermicelli and vegetables. Increase the heat and vigorously toss the ingredients in the wok until they are evenly combined and very hot. Season with salt and pepper to taste. Turn into a warmed serving bowl and garnish with parsley leaves. Serve at once.

Peppers can be stuffed with many different combinations of
ingredients. Try adding chopped anchovies, cooked chicken
or bacon to the filling.

stuffed peppers

4	Serves
10 minutes	Preparation time
about **1 1/4** hours	Cooking time
315	Kcal
1330	KJ
12 g	Protein
5 g	Fat
59 g	CHO

1 Bring the water to the boil with 1/2 teaspoon salt, add the rice and cook for 30 minutes, until the rice is tender and all the water has been absorbed.

300 ml/1/2 pint water
175 g/6 oz brown rice
4 tomatoes, skinned and chopped
1 onion, grated
25 g/1 oz seedless raisins
75 g/3 oz low-fat Cheddar cheese, grated
2 tablespoons chopped parsley
pinch of ground cinnamon
4 red or green peppers, halved, cored and deseeded, with stalks left intact
5 tablespoons Vegetable Stock (see page 6)
salt and pepper

2 When the rice is cooked, remove from the heat and gently stir in the tomatoes, onion and raisins. Stir in two-thirds of the cheese, then the parsley and cinnamon and season to taste with salt and pepper.

3 Arrange the pepper halves, cut side up, in an ovenproof dish. Divide the rice mixture equally among them and sprinkle the remaining cheese over the top. Pour the stock around the peppers and cover with foil. Bake in a preheated oven, 200°C (400° F), Gas Mark 6, for 30–40 minutes, or until tender.

peperonata
with wholewheat noodles

Serves	**6**
Preparation time	**20-25** minutes
Cooking time	**20** minutes
Kcal	**170**
KJ	**720**
Protein	**6** g
Fat	**5** g
CHO	**28** g

2 tablespoons olive oil

1 large onion, thinly sliced

1 large garlic clove, crushed

2 red peppers, cored, deseeded and cut into strips

2 green peppers, cored, deseeded and cut into strips

375 g/12 oz tomatoes, skinned, deseeded and chopped

1 tablespoon chopped basil

175 g/6 oz wholewheat noodles

salt and pepper

basil sprigs, to garnish

1 Heat 1 tablespoon of the olive oil in a deep frying pan. Add the onion and garlic and cook very gently until the onion is soft but not coloured. Add the peppers, tomatoes, basil and salt and pepper to taste. Cover and cook gently for 10 minutes.

2 Remove the lid from the pan and cook over fairly high heat until most of the moisture has evaporated. Keep the vegetable mixture warm.

3 Meanwhile, cook the noodles in plenty of boiling salted water until just tender. Drain the noodles thoroughly and toss in the remaining olive oil. Add salt and pepper to taste.

4 Divide the noodles among 4 serving plates and spoon the hot peperonata over the top. Garnish with sprigs of fresh basil and serve immediately, as a light main course with a salad.

Peperonata is a classic summer dish, combining the best of summer produce – peppers, fresh tomatoes and fresh basil. Use fresh wholewheat noodles if you can – these take about 8–10 minutes to cook, but the extra time is well worth it for the flavour.

The salads in this chapter combine contrasting colours and textures with low-fat dressings. Some make a meal in themselves, while others are interesting side dishes.

salads and side dishes

Celeriac is a root vegetable which resembles a large, knobbly turnip. It has a sweet, nutty celery flavour.

celeriac
and carrot remoulade

4 as a side salad	Serves
20 minutes	Preparation time
10 minutes	Cooking time
94	Kcal
390	KJ
4 g	Protein
4 g	Fat
11 g	CHO

1 celeriac root,
   about 250 g/8 oz,
   sliced into matchstick
   strips
2 tablespoons lemon juice
250 g/8 oz carrots, sliced
   into matchstick strips
salt

dressing:

4 tablespoons low-fat
   mayonnaise
150 ml/¼ pint very low-fat
   natural yogurt
1 garlic clove, crushed
1 tablespoon chopped
   parsley
1 tablespoon finely
   snipped chives
½ teaspoon mustard powder
pinch of cayenne pepper

to garnish:

1 hard-boiled egg,
   chopped
snipped chives

1 Drop the celeriac strips as you cut them into a bowl of water with 1 tablespoon of the lemon juice.

2 Partly cook the celeriac and carrot strips for 5–8 minutes in boiling salted water with the remaining lemon juice. Drain, dry on kitchen paper and leave to cool.

3 To make the dressing, mix the ingredients in a bowl. Taste and adjust the seasoning if necessary.

4 Toss the celeriac and carrots in the dressing and spoon the salad on to a serving dish. Garnish with the hard-boiled egg and chives and serve.

smoked chicken
and fruit salad

serves	**8**
Preparation time	**25** minutes
Kcal	**116**
KJ	**485**
Protein	**11** g
Fat	**5** g
CHO	**6** g

1 lettuce, shredded

2 celery sticks, chopped

**1 red pepper, cored,
deseeded and sliced**

25 g/1 oz walnut halves

**75 g/3 oz green grapes,
peeled, halved
and deseeded**

**1 pear, peeled, cored
and sliced**

**250 g/8 oz smoked chicken,
skinned, boned and cut
into strips**

dressing:

**2 tablespoons low-fat
natural yogurt**

**2 tablespoons low-fat
mayonnaise**

**2 tablespoons grated
cucumber**

1 teaspoon grated onion

**½ teaspoon chopped
tarragon**

salt and pepper

to garnish:

1 pear, cored and sliced

tarragon sprigs

1 In a large salad bowl, mix the lettuce with the celery, red pepper, walnuts, grapes, pear and smoked chicken.

2 Mix the yogurt with the mayonnaise, cucumber, onion and tarragon, blending well. Add salt and pepper to taste.

3 Just before serving, spoon the dressing over the salad ingredients and toss well to mix.

4 Garnish with slices of pear and a few sprigs of fresh tarragon.

Any leftover smoked chicken will keep well and can be
used in sandwiches. Use the bones to flavour stock.

caponata

Serves	**6**
Preparation time	**20** minutes
Cooking time	**1** hour **20** minutes
Kcal	**74**
KJ	**313**
Protein	**3** g
Fat	**4** g
CHO	**7** g

2 tablespoons olive oil

1 onion, thinly sliced

2 celery sticks, diced

3 aubergines cut into
1 cm/½ inch dice

150 ml/¼ pint passata

3 tablespoons wine vinegar

1 yellow pepper, cored,
deseeded and
thinly sliced

1 red pepper, cored,
deseeded and
thinly sliced

25 g/1 oz anchovy fillets,
soaked in warm water,
drained and dried

50 g/2 oz capers,
roughly chopped

25 g/1 oz black olives,
pitted and sliced

25 g/1 oz green olives,
pitted and sliced

2 tablespoons chopped
parsley, to serve

1 Heat the oil in a saucepan, add the onion and sauté until soft and golden. Add the celery and cook for 2–3 minutes. Add the aubergine and cook gently for 3 minutes, stirring occasionally.

2 Add the passata and cook gently until it has been absorbed. Add the wine vinegar and cook for 1 minute. Add the peppers, anchovies, capers and olives and cook for 3 minutes.

3 Transfer the mixture to an ovenproof dish and bake, covered, in a preheated oven, 180°C (350°F), Gas Mark 4, for about 1 hour. Serve lukewarm or cold sprinkled with chopped parsley.

This aubergine dish originated in Sicily. Serve on its own with crusty bread as a light meal, or as an accompaniment to plain grilled fish or chicken.

It is important to indulge oneself, even when on a low-fat diet. These desserts are surprisingly low in fat. Many are fruit based, bursting with tempting colours and juicy flavours.

desserts

orange
diet cheesecake

Serves	**10**
Preparation time	**15** minutes, plus chilling
Kcal	**128**
KJ	**536**
Protein	**10** g
Fat	**5** g
CHO	**11** g

**40 g/1½ oz low-fat
   spread, softened
8 digestive biscuits,
   crushed
125 g/4 oz very low-fat
   cottage cheese
4 tablespoons skimmed milk
375 g/12 oz quark cheese
3 tablespoons orange juice
grated rind of 2 oranges
artificial liquid sweetener,
   to taste
2 eggs, separated
15 g/½ oz powdered
   gelatine
3 tablespoons water
4 large oranges**

1 Lightly grease an 18 cm/ 7 inch loose-bottomed cake tin with a little of the low-fat spread. Mix the remaining spread with the biscuit crumbs. Spoon evenly over the base of the cake tin and press down firmly with the back of a wooden spoon.

2 Meanwhile, purée the cottage cheese and milk in a blender until smooth. Mix together the quark, cottage cheese mixture, orange juice, three-quarters of the rind and artificial sweetener to taste. Beat the egg yolks into the mixture, one at a time, beating well after each addition.

3 Sprinkle the gelatine over the water in a small heatproof bowl and leave for a few minutes until spongy. Place the bowl in a saucepan of hot water and stir over a very gentle heat until dissolved. Allow to cool slightly, then stir into the cheese mixture. Chill in the refrigerator until thick and just beginning to set. Whisk the egg whites stiffly, then fold them into the cheese mixture, using a large metal spoon.

4 Pour the cheese mixture over the crumb base. Smooth the surface and chill in the refrigerator for about 5 hours until set.

5 Peel and divide the oranges into segments. Decorate the top edge of the cheesecake with the larger, better-looking slices and sprinkle the centre with the remaining rind.

summer pudding

Serves	**4**
Preparation time	**30** minutes, plus chilling
Cooking time	**3** minutes
Kcal	**150**
KJ	**620**
Protein	**5** g
Fat	**1** g
CHO	**30** g

**250 g/8 oz red and white
currants**
125 g/4 oz blackcurrants
125 g/4 oz raspberries
125 g/4 oz loganberries
125 g/4 oz strawberries
**125 g/4 oz cherries,
blueberries or cultivated
blackberries**
**1 tablespoon clear honey
margarine, for greasing**
**8 x 1 cm/½ inch thick
slices brown bread,
crusts removed**

1 Place all the fruit in a
large saucepan (it must not
be aluminium or cast iron)
with the honey and cook very
gently for 2–3 minutes, just
long enough to soften the
fruit and allow the juices to
run a little.

2 Line a lightly greased 1.2
litre/2 pint pudding basin with
three-quarters of the bread,
trimming the slices to fit,
making certain that all the
surfaces are completely
covered and the base has
an extra thick layer.

3 Spoon in all the fruit,
reserving 2 tablespoons of
the juice in case the bread is
not completely coloured by
the fruit when the pudding is
turned out. Cover with the
remaining bread. Lay a plate
or saucepan lid that will fit
inside the rim of the bowl on
top and place a 1 kg/2 lb
weight on top of the plate or
lid. Chill for 10–12 hours.

4 Turn out and cut into
wedges to serve.

This classic English pudding is made with a selection
of summer soft fruits which you can vary as you
choose. Use one of the softer, lighter types of brown
bread for this recipe.

peach granita

4	Serves
20–25 minutes, plus chilling	Preparation time
5 minutes	Cooking time
70	Kcal
290	KJ
2 g	Protein
1 g	Fat
9 g	CHO

**375 g/12 oz fresh ripe
peaches**

**150 ml/¼ pint dry
white wine**

**150 ml/¼ pint fresh
orange juice**

2 egg whites

1 Nick the stalk end of each peach. Plunge into a bowl of boiling water for 30–45 seconds, then slide off the skins. Halve the fruit, removing the stones, and chop the flesh roughly.

2 Put the peach flesh into a pan with the white wine and orange juice. Simmer gently for 5 minutes.

3 Blend the peaches and the liquid in a food processor or blender until smooth. Cool.

4 Pour into a shallow freezer container and freeze until the granita is slushy around the edges, then tip into a bowl and break up the ice crystals.

5 Whisk the egg whites until stiff but not dry. Fold lightly but thoroughly into the partly-frozen granita, return to the container and freeze until firm.

To remove the stones from the peaches, slice them in half around the stone, through the groove, and twist the two halves to separate. Lever the stone out with a knife.

There is no need to grease tins when cooking this type
of pastry because of the high fat content of the dough.
In some other recipes the tins may need to be greased.

french apple flan

10	Serves
15 minutes, plus chilling	Preparation time
35–40	Cooking time
211	Kcal
889	KJ
3 g	Protein
5 g	Fat
41 g	CHO

1 kg/2 lb cooking apples,
   peeled, cored, thinly
   sliced and puréed
2 red-skinned dessert
   apples, thinly sliced
50 g/2 oz caster sugar
4 tablespoons apricot jam
2 tablespoons lemon juice

pâte sucrée:
150 g/5 oz plain flour
50 g/2 oz butter
50 g/2 oz caster sugar
1 egg and 1 egg white,
   beaten together
few drops vanilla essence

1 To make the pâte sucrée, sift the flour on to a cool work surface. Make a well in the centre and add the butter, sugar, egg and egg white and vanilla essence. Using the fingertips of one hand, work these ingredients together, then draw in the flour. Knead lightly until smooth, then cover and chill for 1 hour.

2 Roll out the pastry very thinly on a floured work surface and use to line a 25 cm/10 inch fluted flan ring. Fill the case generously with the apple purée, then arrange an overlapping layer of sliced apples on top. Sprinkle with the sugar. Bake in a preheated oven, 190°C (375°F), Gas Mark 5, for 35–40 minutes.

3 Meanwhile, heat the jam with the lemon juice, then strain and brush over the apples. Serve hot or cold.

strawberry ice

Serves	**4**
Preparation time	**25** minutes, plus freezing
Kcal	**126**
KJ	**525**
Protein	**7** g
Fat	**5** g
CHO	**14** g

3 egg yolks
1 tablespoon redcurrant
jelly
1 tablespoon red vermouth
300 ml/½ pint natural
yogurt
375 g/12 oz ripe
strawberries, hulled
4–6 strawberries, with
stalks, halved, to
decorate

1 Put the egg yolks into a blender or food processor with the redcurrant jelly, vermouth, yogurt and half the strawberries and blend until smooth.

2 Transfer the mixture to a shallow freezerproof container, and freeze until the ice cream starts to harden around the edges.

3 Tip the ice cream into a bowl and beat to break up the ice crystals.

4 Chop the remaining strawberries and mix them into the half-frozen ice cream. Return the ice cream to the container and freeze until quite firm.

5 Scoop the ice cream into stemmed glasses and decorate each one with strawberry halves.

Yogurt adds a piquant flavour to ice cream. Eat the ice cream soon after it is frozen before it becomes too hard.

yogurt-fruit cup

6	Serves
10 minutes, plus chilling	Preparation time
124	Kcal
526	KJ
4 g	Protein
3 g	Fat
23 g	CHO

**500 g/1 lb can sliced
peaches or sliced pears
in fruit juice, drained**
**475 ml/16 fl oz low-fat
vanilla yogurt**

1 Divide the sliced peaches
or sliced pears evenly among
6 small glass dessert bowls,
in layers.

to decorate:
**2 tablespoons finely
chopped toasted almonds**
**½ teaspoon ground
cardamom, to garnish**

2 Top each bowl with an
equal quantity of the yogurt
and chill in the refrigerator
until required.

3 To serve, sprinkle each
bowl lightly with the toasted
almonds and garnish with
ground cardamom.

This recipe offers a new twist to a back-to-basics
favourite. It is ideal for preparing in advance and you'll
like the fragrant touch of cardamom. It would also make
a refreshing breakfast alternative, by substituting the
almonds with muesli.

Acknowledgements

Octopus Publishing Group Ltd./Martin Brigdale 30.
/Philip Dowell 41. /Gus Filgate 22-23. /Diana Miller 9.
/Hilary Moore 7, 25, 39, 44. /James Murphy 24, 34, 37.
/Simon Smith 3, 10, 13, 15, 17, 18, 21, 27, 29, 33.

This edition first published in 1999 for S.T.I.S. by Hamlyn
an imprint of Octopus Publishing Group Ltd
2-4 Heron Quays, London E14 4JP

Material used in this book first appeared in
Low Fat Cooking published by Hamlyn in 1999

ISBN 0 600 59996 5